The
Pied Piper
Of Hamelin

A Life-Lesson

(well-earned and well-learned)

In Rhyme

Robert Browning's

~

The
Pied Piper
Of Hamelin

Illustrations by

Bud Peen

Harry N. Abrams, Inc.
Publishers

I.

amelin Town's in Brunswick,
    By famous Hanover city.
        The river Weser, deep and wide,
Washes its walls on the southern side.
A pleasanter spot you never spied.
But, when begins my ditty,
Almost five hundred years ago,
To see the townsfolk suffer so
From vermin, was a pity.

II.

Rats!

They fought the dogs and killed the cats,

And bit the babies in the cradles,

And ate the cheeses out of the vats,

And licked the soup from the cooks' own ladles,

Split open the kegs of salted sprats,

Made nests inside men's Sunday hats,

And even spoiled the women's chats

By drowning their speaking

With shrieking and squeaking

In fifty different sharps and flats.

III.

At last the people in a body
To the Town Hall came flocking.
"'Tis clear," cried they, "our Mayor's noddy,
And as for our Corporation — shocking
To think we buy gowns lined with ermine
For dolts that can't or won't determine
What's best to rid us of our vermin!
You hope, because you're old and obese,
To find in the furry civic robe ease?
Rouse up, sirs! Give your brains a racking
To find the remedy we're lacking,
Or, sure as fate, we'll send you packing!"
At this the Mayor and Corporation
Quaked with a mighty consternation.

IV.

An hour they sat in council.

At length the Mayor broke silence,

"For a guilder I'd my ermine gown sell,

I wish I were a mile hence!

It's easy to bid one rack one's brain,

I'm sure my poor head aches again,

I've scratched it so, and all in vain.

Oh for a trap, a trap, a trap!"

Just as he said this, what should hap?

At the chamber door but a gentle tap.

"Bless us," cried the Mayor, "what's that?"

(With the Corporation as he sat,

Looking little, though wondrous fat.

Nor brighter was his eye, nor moister

Than a too-long-opened oyster,

Save when at noon his paunch grew mutinous

For a plate of turtle green and glutinous.)

"Only a scraping of shoes on the mat?

Anything like the sound of a rat

Makes my heart go pit-a-pat!"

V.

"Come in!" the Mayor cried, looking bigger.

And in did come the strangest figure!

His queer long coat from heel to head

Was half of yellow and half of red.

And he himself was tall and thin,

With sharp blue eyes, each like a pin.

And light loose hair, yet swarthy skin,

No tuft on cheek nor beard on chin,

But lips where smiles went out and in.

There was no guessing his kith and kin.

And nobody could enough admire

The tall man and his quaint attire.

Quoth one, "It's as my great-grandsire,

Starting up at The Trump of Doom's tone,

Had walked this way from his painted tombstone!"

VI.

He advanced to the council-table
And, "Please your honors," said he, "I'm able,
By means of a secret charm, to draw
All creatures living beneath the sun,
That creep or swim or fly or run,
After me so as you never saw!
And I chiefly use my charm
On creatures that do people harm —
The mole and toad and newt and viper.
And people call me the Pied Piper."
(And here they noticed around his neck
A scarf of red and yellow stripe,
To match with his coat of the self-same check.

And at the scarf's end hung a pipe.
And his fingers, they noticed, were ever straying
As if impatient to be playing
Upon this pipe, as low it dangled
Over his vesture so old fangled.)
"Yet," said he, "poor piper as I am,
In Tartary I freed the Cham,
Last June, from his huge swarms of gnats;
I eased in Asia the Nizam
Of a monstrous brood of vampire bats.
And as for what your brain bewilders,
If I can rid your town of rats
Will you give me a thousand guilders?"
"One? fifty thousand!" was the exclamation
Of the astonished Mayor and Corporation.

VII. *Into the street the Piper stept,*
Smiling first a little smile,
As if he knew what magic slept
In his quiet pipe the while.
Then, like a musical adept,
To blow the pipe his lips he wrinkled,
And green and blue his sharp eyes twinkled,
Like a candle flame where salt is sprinkled.
And ere three shrill notes the pipe uttered,
You heard as if an army muttered.

And the muttering grew to a grumbling,
And the grumbling grew to a mighty rumbling,
And out of the houses the rats came tumbling.
Great rats, small rats, lean rats, brawny rats,
Brown rats, black rats, grey rats, tawny rats,
Grave old plodders, gay young friskers,
Fathers, mothers, uncles, cousins,
Cocking tails and pricking whiskers,
Families by tens and dozens,
Brothers, sisters, husbands, wives,
Followed the Piper for their lives.
From street to street he piped advancing,
And step for step they followed dancing,
Until they came to the river Weser,
Wherein all plunged and perished!
— Save one who, stout as Julius Caesar,
Swam across and lived to carry
(As he the manuscript he cherished)
To Rat Land home, his commentary.

Which was: "At the first shrill notes of the pipe,
I heard a sound as of scraping tripe,
And putting apples, wondrous ripe,
Into a cider press's gripe;
And a moving away of pickle-tub boards,
And a leaving ajar of conserve cupboards,
And a drawing the corks of train-oil flasks,
And a breaking the hoops of butter casks.
And it seemed as if a voice
(Sweeter far than by harp or by psaltery
Is breathed) called out, 'Oh rats, rejoice!
The world is grown to one vast drysaltery!
So munch on, crunch on, take your nuncheon,
Breakfast, supper, dinner, luncheon!'
And just as bulky sugar-puncheon
Already staved, like a great sun shone
Glorious scarce an inch before me —
Just as methought it said, 'Come, bore me!'
I found the Weser rolling o'er me."

VIII.

You should have heard the Hamelin people
Ringing the bells till they rocked the steeple.
"Go," cried the Mayor, "and get long poles,
Poke out the nests and block up the holes!
Consult with carpenters and builders,
And leave in our town not even a trace
Of the rats!" — When suddenly, up the face
Of the Piper perked in the market-place,
With a, "First, if you please, my thousand guilders!"

IX.

A thousand guilders! The Mayor looked blue,
So did the Corporation too.
For council dinners made rare havoc
With Claret, Moselle, Vin-de-Grave, Hock;
And half the money would replenish
Their cellar's biggest butt with Rhenish.
To pay this sum to a wandering fellow
With a gypsy coat of red and yellow!
"Beside," quoth the Mayor with a knowing wink,
"Our business was done all at the river's brink."

All the little boys and girls,
With rosy cheeks and flaxen curls,
And sparkling eyes and teeth like pearls,
Tripping and skipping, ran merrily after
The wonderful music with shouting and laughter.

XIII. The Mayor was dumb, and the Council stood
As if they were changed into blocks of wood,
Unable to move a step, or cry
To the children merrily skipping by,
And could only follow with the eye
That joyous crowd at the Piper's back.
But how the Mayor was on the rack,
And the wretched Council's bosoms beat,
As the Piper turned from the High Street
To where the Weser rolled its waters
Right in the way of their sons and daughters!
However he turned from South to West
And to Koppelberg Hill his steps addressed,
And after him the children pressed.
Great was the joy in every breast.

"He never can cross that mighty top!
He's forced to let the piping drop,
And we shall see our children stop!"
When, lo, as they reached the mountain side,
A wondrous portal opened wide,
As if a cavern was suddenly hollowed.
And the Piper advanced and the children followed.
And when all were in to the very last,
The door in the mountain side shut fast.
Did I say all? No! One was lame
And could not dance the whole of the way.
And in after years, if you would blame
His sadness, he was used to say,
"It's dull in our town since my playmates left!
I can't forget that I'm bereft
Of all the pleasant sights they see,
Which the Piper also promised me.

For he led us, he said, to a joyous land,

Joining the town and just at hand

Where waters gushed and fruit trees grew,

And flowers put forth a fairer hue,

And everything was strange and new.

The sparrows were brighter than peacocks here,

And their dogs outran our fallow deer,

And honeybees had lost their stings,

And horses were born with eagles' wings.

And just as I became assured

My lame foot would be speedily cured,

The music stopped and I stood still,

And found myself outside the hill,

Left alone against my will

To go now limping as before,

And never hear of that country more!"

XIV.

Alas, alas for Hamelin!

There came into many a burgher's pate

A text which says that Heaven's Gate

Opes to the rich at as easy rate

As the needle's eye takes a camel in!

The Mayor sent East, West, North and South

To offer the Piper, by word of mouth,

Wherever it was men's lot to find him,

Silver and gold to his heart's content,

If he'd only return the way he went,

And bring the children behind him.

But when they saw 'twas a lost endeavor,

And Piper and dancers were gone forever,

They made a decree that lawyers never

Should think their records dated duly

If, after the day of the month and year,

These words did not as well appear:
"And so long after what happened here
On the Twenty-second of July,
Thirteen hundred and seventy-six."
And the better in memory to fix
The place of the children's last retreat,
They called it the Pied Piper's Street,
Where anyone playing on pipe or tabor
Was sure for the future to lose his labor.
Nor suffered they hostelry or tavern
To shock with mirth a street so solemn.
But opposite the place of the cavern
They wrote the story on a column.
And on the great church window painted
The same, to make the world acquainted
How their children were stolen away,
And there it stands to this very day.

And I must not omit to say
That in Transylvania there's a tribe
Of alien people who ascribe
The outlandish ways and dress
On which their neighbors lay such stress,
To their fathers and mothers having risen
Out of some subterraneous prison
Into which they were trepanned
Long time ago in a mighty band
Out of Hamelin town in Brunswick Land —
But how or why, they don't understand.

XV.

o, Willy, let me and you be wipers
Of scores out with all men,
Especially pipers!
And, whether they pipe us free
From rats or from mice,
If we've promised them aught —
Let us keep our promise!

F⬚Y
PRODUCTIONS

The Pied Piper of Hamelin was edited, designed, and electronically produced by
Fly Productions, San Francisco.

[EDITOR'S NOTE] We referred to two sources for this edition of *The Pied Piper of Hamelin:* the
well-known British edition, illustrated by Kate Greenaway, published in 1888, and a less-known
edition, designed and illustrated in London by Arthur C. Payne and Harry Payne, printed in
Munich, and published c.1896 in New York by The Art Lithographic Publishing Company.
(The presentation of the work in both was nearly identical.) We have taken some editorial
liberties, however, adapting the punctuation and spelling to welcome our modern-day readers, and
adding an epigram – just for fun – on the page opposite the title. In all other ways, this edition
of Mr. Browning's poem remains as he penned it over one hundred and fifty years ago.

LIBRARY OF CONGRESS CATALOGING-IN-PUBLICATION DATA
BROWNING, ROBERT, 1812–1889.
THE PIED PIPER OF HAMELIN : POEM / BY ROBERT BROWNING ; ILLUSTRATED BY BUD PEEN.
P.   CM.
SUMMARY: THE PIED PIPER PIPES THE VILLAGE FREE OF RATS, AND WHEN THE VILLAGERS
REFUSE TO PAY HIM FOR THE SERVICE HE EXACTS A TERRIBLE REVENGE.
ISBN 0-8109-4351-4
1. PIED PIPER OF HAMELIN (LEGENDARY CHARACTER) — JUVENILE POETRY.
2. CHILDREN'S POETRY, ENGLISH.   [1. PIED PIPER OF HAMELIN
(LEGENDARY CHARACTER) — POETRY.   2. FOLKLORE — GERMANY — HAMELN — POETRY.
3. ENGLISH POETRY.]   I. PEEN, BUD   II. TITLE.
PR4222.P5   1999
821'.8 — DC21   98–43395

HARRY N. ABRAMS, INC.
100 FIFTH AVENUE
NEW YORK, N.Y. 10011
WWW.ABRAMSBOOKS.COM